To Emily
on your 18th
Birthday.

With
Love
From

The Sandy Family
xxx
xx

C.S. LEWIS
ON POLITICS, GOVERNMENT, AND THE GOOD SOCIETY

*Relevant insights and sage wisdom
for contemporary Christians*

Jefrey D. Breshears

C. S. Lewis on Politics, Government, and the Good Society

Copyright 2020 by Jefrey D. Breshears

Centre•Pointe Publishing. A division of The Areopagus, Inc.
www.TheAreopagus.org

All rights reserved. No part of this publication may be reproduced, stored in a retrieval system, or transmitted in any form by an means, electronic, mechanical, photocopy, or otherwise, without the prior permission of the publisher, except as provided by USA copyright law.

ISBN: 9781678572594

Thanks to **Andrea Smith** for production assistance.

Thanks to **Pamela Phillips, Randall Hough, David Ott** and **George Weaver** for your editorial assistance and critical feedback in the preparation and revisions of this manuscript. Your perceptive critiques and suggestions are much appreciated.

*To my friends and colleagues in
The Areopagus,
and to all thinking Christians
who conscientiously endeavor
to love and serve God with all their
heart, soul, mind, and strength.
You are indeed the light of the world
and the salt of the earth.*

C. S. LEWIS
ON POLITICS, GOVERNMENT, AND THE GOOD SOCIETY

"I believe in Christianity as I believe that the sun has risen, not only because I see it, but because by it I see everything else."
– C. S. Lewis, "Is Theology Poetry?"

INTRODUCTION

C. S. Lewis is generally regarded as the foremost Christian thinker and writer of the Twentieth Century. A first-rate scholar, philosopher, apologist, theologian, literary critic, science fiction writer, poet, and author of children's fantasy novels, he wrote with charm, wit, insight, and occasional eloquence. More than fifty years after his death on November 22, 1963, thirty-six of his books are still in print, and collectively they have sold nearly 275 million copies worldwide. In 2000 *Christianity Today* magazine voted *Mere Christianity*, his informal primer in Christian apologetics, the most influential Christian book of the century, while *The Chronicles of Narnia* was #2 and *The Screwtape Letters* #3 on the list.* Walter Hooper, who served briefly as Lewis' private secretary and later as a co-executor of his literary estate, referred to Lewis as "the most

---

* https://www.goodreads.com/list/show/13084._Christianity_Today_Books_of_the_20th_Century.

thoroughly converted man I ever met" whose "whole vision of life was such that the natural and supernatural seemed inseparably combined."* In light of his ongoing legacy and influence, Lewis might well be regarded as one of the twenty most significant and influential Christians in history.

As a theologically orthodox Christian writing in a post-Christian age, Lewis offered a scathing critique of "liberal Christianity" and modern secular humanism and their destructive effects on the spiritual and moral culture in Great Britain and other Western societies. Like G. K. Chesterton and his friend and colleague, J. R. R. Tolkien, Lewis' writings were self-consciously and deliberately out of synch with modern trends and fads. Paradoxically, because his writings address the perennial issues of life – the True, the Good, and the Beautiful – they are timeless and perpetually relevant. Furthermore, as a logical apologist who came to faith through the influence of imaginative myth, Lewis appeals both to rationalists and romantics alike.

Although no average man, in some respects Lewis serves as the Everyman of the modern age. In his life, Lewis' intellectual and spiritual pilgrimage was an existential journey through many of the Twentieth Century's major philosophical themes:

- From nominal Christianity to atheistic skepticism.
- From atheistic skepticism to romantic idealism.
- From romantic idealism to Theosophical Occultism.
- From Theosophical Occultism to pantheism.
- From pantheism to Manichaeism.
- From Manichaeism to generic theism.
- From generic theism to Christianity.

* In this study I provide full citations for lengthy quotations but not for most short quotations so as to avoid cluttering the text with excessive footnotes.

Lewis was a "mere Christian" – a "Great Tradition Christian" as he preferred to describe himself – and as such he appeals to believers across theological and denominational lines. Convinced that sectarianism is one of the Devil's most effective weapons against Christianity, what mattered most to Lewis were the core defining doctrines of the Christian faith: the Trinity, the deity of Christ, the Incarnation, the Atonement, the Resurrection, and the doctrinal and moral authority of Scripture. As the Lewis scholar Louis Markos has noted, "Lewis was boldly orthodox but generously ecumenical," appealing to traditional Protestants, Anabaptists and Roman Catholics alike.

Most notably, those who knew him best attested to his character and integrity. At Lewis' memorial service following his death on November 22, 1963, one eulogist described him as "the best-read man any of us is ever likely to meet," while another called him "perhaps the most brilliant man in the world." One Lewis biographer, George Sayer, noted that his "flow of wit, humour, and vivid stories told in his deep, rich voice was inexhaustible," and lauded him "a man of his word, a man of integrity, and a man of honour" whose conversion to Christianity had altered him radically. According to the renowned conservative Anglican pastor, John R.W. Stott, Lewis was "a Christ-centered, great-tradition mainstream Christian whose stature a generation after his death seems greater than anyone ever thought while he was alive, and whose Christian writings are now seen as having classic status." In a *Christianity Today* interview prior to the release of the movie version of *The Lion, the Witch, and the Wardrobe* in 2003, Douglas Gresham spoke of Lewis as "the finest man and the best Christian I've ever known," adding, "I don't know of any major vice that Jack took to his grave."

As a "mere Christian" who sought to honor God with all his heart, soul, mind, and strength, Lewis serves as an example for us all. As the philosopher and theologian Clement of Alexandria (c. 150-215) taught, every devout Christian should aspire to be a

Bible scholar, a theologian, a philosopher, a contemplative practitioner, and a Christian apologist. Lewis embodied all these attributes, and as such he serves in many ways as a model for Christian maturity. A case might also be made that Lewis was perhaps the Twentieth Century's preeminent sage – a man who integrated an astonishing breadth and depth of knowledge with profound wisdom.

C. S. Lewis was neither a professional philosopher, theologian, Bible scholar, historian, psychologist, nor a social scientist, but he thought and wrote perceptively on all these subjects. A rarity among intellectuals, he integrated both reason and imagination into his life and works. Lewis understood that unless conditioned by humility and Christian discipline, reason tends to solidify into sterile Rationalism while imagination tends to drift toward idealistic Romanticism. Therefore, Christian maturity necessitates a thoughtful and faithful integration of both mind and heart.

Although Lewis' writings on political philosophy are often overlooked and he is seldom regarded as an authority on matters related to modern political science, he was in fact as acute and perceptive in this vital area of life as in other aspects of Christian discipleship. Lewis understood that Christianity is more than a religion and more than personal piety. As a life-transforming relationship with God via faith in Jesus Christ, the Christian faith is a lifestyle and a comprehensive worldview that should encompass all the pertinent issues of life including one's social and political convictions.

To that end, this study focuses on three component aspects of Lewis' views on the proper role and scope of government and Christian citizenship responsibilities based on his understanding of human nature and the reality of a transcendent moral law:

    I. Natural Law: The Moral Foundation for Government
    II. The Political Philosophy of C. S. Lewis
    III. Ruminations on the "Good Society"

I. NATURAL LAW:
THE MORAL FOUNDATION FOR GOVERNMENT

The *Tao* and the Platonic Triad

The best introduction to Lewis' political philosophy is his book, *The Abolition of Man*, published in 1944 and distilled from a series of lectures he delivered at the University of Durham the previous year. Inspired in part by G. K. Chesterton's classic work, *The Everlasting Man*, Lewis' *The Abolition of Man* is an astute analysis of the philosophical and moral decline of the West – how and why the modern world has gone wrong. As such, the book functions as a primer for everything else Lewis wrote on the state of Western civilization and culture, including politics. At the same time that Hitler and Stalin were terrorizing humanity, prominent philosophers such as A. J. Ayer and Bertrand Russell promoted moral relativism and sowed the seeds of what would later be termed postmodernism.

Lewis begins with a basic *a priori* premise – the ancient Chinese concept of the *Tao* (pronounced *Dao*: "The Way") – or the natural order of things. Lewis correlates the moral and social aspects of the *Tao* with traditional Natural Law theory* and cites various law codes in ancient, medieval and early-modern cultures that support the premise of a universal code of ethics. As the term is used in philosophy, theology, and the social sciences, Natural Law constitutes the moral and

---

* In this text I capitalize "Natural Law" for the purpose of emphasis and to distinguish this moral tradition from the natural (physical) laws that regulate the universe.

ethical precepts that are an integral part of our human inheritance and which we sense intuitively as a result of being made in the *imago Dei* (the "image of God"). These axioms are self-evident, and they are the source from which all moral judgments come. They also function as expressions of moral-based common sense derived from ethical principles that are essential to social harmony in any truly civilized society. As such, these moral maxims can be summarized in one simple concept: "Do good and avoid evil."

In the history of philosophy the concept of Natural Law has sometimes been called the "perennial philosophy," and in *The Abolition of Man* Lewis explains its significance this way:

> This thing which I have called for convenience the *Tao*, and which others may call Natural Law or Traditional Morality... is not one among a series of possible systems of value. It is the sole source of all value judgements. If it is rejected, all value is rejected. [C. S. Lewis, *The Abolition of Man*, p. 43.]

Lewis proceeds to make the case for the universal awareness of Natural Law based on mankind's inherent rational capacity. That being the case, these moral and ethical precepts are, as the Christian philosopher J. Budziszewski declares, "what we can't not know." Furthermore, they are so obvious and commonsensical that in order to violate them one must intentionally deny both their reality as well as their validity. As Gilbert Meilander explains in his book, *The Taste for the Other*, these moral imperatives are true because they correlate to the realities of human nature:

> In the *Tao* we have objective moral knowledge, for it expresses truths about human nature. These truths about human nature provide the first principles for moral reasoning.... Hence, for Lewis the basic imperatives of morality are grounded in the structure of reality.... Moral knowledge is knowledge of reality – of what is natural for man. [Gilbert Meilander, *The Taste for the Other: The Social and Ethical Thought of C. S. Lewis*, pp. 197, 203.]

To reiterate, these truths are self-evident, and those who refuse to acknowledge them typically do so out of moral rebellion rather than ignorance. Although such persons may claim to be "open-minded" or "progressive," they are in reality intellectually dishonest in their refusal to concede that these moral values are indisputable, as Lewis explains:

> This is what Confucius meant when he said, "With those who follow a different Way it is useless to take counsel." This is why Aristotle said that only those who have been well brought up can usefully study ethics....
>
> An open mind, in questions that are not ultimate, is useful. But an open mind about the ultimate foundations either of Theoretical or of Practical Reason is idiocy. If a man's mind is open on these things, let his mouth at least be shut. [C. S. Lewis, *The Abolition of Man*, pp. 59, 48]

Early in *The Abolition of Man* Lewis focuses on the problem of modern "progressive" education, which he contends is being corrupted by relativistic values. Citing Plato and Aristotle, Lewis stresses that the basic goal of education should be to train the mind to think clearly and morally so as to develop good habits – i.e., "to make the pupil like and dislike what he ought." Virtue must become a passion, and in that regard it is imperative that our soul be conditioned in such a way that reason rules emotions. To fulfill our God-given calling as human beings, we must learn to love what is commonly referred to as the Platonic triad: The True, the Good, and the Beautiful. Correspondingly, we must learn to despise what is untrue, evil, and ugly. According to Lewis, "A right response to the problems of life is not something automatically present in our [human] nature." In reality, it involves "a delicate balance of trained habits, laboriously acquired and easily lost." But without the aid of trained emotions, "the intellect is powerless against the animal organism." Furthermore, it should be emphasized that the Platonic triad applies as much to aesthetics, art, music and imaginative literature as to philosophy, morality and ethics.

However, Lewis observes, the concept of moral absolutes is no longer generally accepted. In fact, much of modern education (not to mention, popular culture) ridicules traditional virtues. This is to  be expected because only those who practice the *Tao* truly understand it. But the problem is that once we eliminate moral absolutes, we abolish man as a moral being and a creature made in the image of God. This is the context in which Lewis employs his metaphor of *"men without chests"* – i.e., without heart and soul – who are driven exclusively by their base instincts and passions. That being the case, the law of the jungle prevails in which might makes right and it's everyone for him/herself in a dog-eat-dog survival of the fittest world. The end result of casting off all moral absolutes is not utopia but dystopia. It also results in the abolition of man as a fully human moral agent. According to Lewis, this was in fact what was going on all over the world with Soviet Communism, German Nazism, Italian Fascism, and Japanese imperialism.

[Note: Significantly, Lewis was one of relatively few academic elites at Oxford who recognized Communism as a threat as diabolical as Nazism.]

In his assessment of the geopolitical crises of the 1930s and '40s, Lewis called attention to the fact that not only politics but religion, philosophy, science, technology, education, and the arts had all being corrupted and exploited by sinister spiritual forces. Furthermore, these secular trends were just as ominous, although more subtle, in democratic societies such as Britain and America as in the USSR and Germany. In his words:

> The process which, if not checked, will abolish Man goes on apace among Communists and Democrats no less than among Fascists. The methods may (at first) differ in brutality. But many a mild-eyed scientist, many a popular dramatist, many an amateur philosopher

[i.e., Darwin, Freud, Shaw, et al.], means in the long run just the same as the Nazi rulers of Germany. Traditional values are to be 'debunked' and mankind to be cut out into some fresh shape at the will of [the elite].... The belief that we can invent "ideologies" at pleasure, and the consequent treatment of mankind as specimens,... begins to affect our very language. Once we killed bad men; now we liquidate unsocial elements [or counter-revolutionaries]. [Ibid., p. 73-74]

[Note: Consider George Orwell's example of Neo-Marxist "Newspeak" in his novel, *1984,* and the fascist alliance of Postmodernism and Political Correctness in contemporary society that imposes secular left-wing speech codes on university campuses and in the offices of corporate America.]

As Lewis explains, one means by which modern man seeks to obscure the *Tao* is by taking one value and making it the preeminent moral and social virtue. For example, Nazism elevated racial and cultural superiority (Aryan nationalism and patriotism) to the highest level over and above all other values, while Communist propaganda extolled the ideal of social equality as the ultimate virtue. Similarly, in our society "tolerance," typically misdefined as unrestricted approval and acceptance, is regarded by liberals and leftists as the premier virtue.

[Note: Ironically, some of the most intolerant people are secular socialists who lecture others – usually Christians and conservatives – on the value of "tolerance". For these sanctimonious apostles of Politically Correctness, "tolerance" is merely a tactic employed to inject their toxic ideas into the bloodstream of mainstream culture. But once such ideologues manage to take control of an institution, they soon prohibit alternative views which they disingenuously label as "hate speech." In reality, they are merely left-wing fascists.]

Lewis implores scientists, both natural scientists and social scientists, to return to a sense of the *Tao* – the natural moral and ethical order of the universe. But what about those whose souls and consciences are so corrupted as to not see or appreciate the True, the

Good, and the Beautiful? What of those *"who call evil good and good evil,"* as the prophet Isaiah described in Isaiah 5:20-21? Such people are morally corrupt, and according to Lewis any attempt to have a moral-based understanding with such an individual is tantamount to trying to have a rational discussion with a madman.

In the Appendix of *The Abolition of Man*, Lewis sets forth some basic core principles of the *Tao* organized according to eight categories:

(1) The Law of General Beneficence. Show proper respect toward all, "Love your neighbour as yourself" (Lev. 19:18), and "Do unto others as you would have them do unto you" (Matt. 7:12).

(2) The Law of Special Beneficence. Love and care for family members: parents, spouse, children and relatives.

(3) Duties to Parents, Elders, and Ancestors.

(4) Duties to Children and Posterity.

(5) The Law of Justice. Equal justice under the law.

(6) The Law of Good Faith and Veracity. Honesty and truthfulness in one's relations with others.

(7) The Law of Mercy. Care for the poor, the sick, widows, orphans, the elderly, and others with special needs.

(8) The Law of Magnanimity. Courage and honor in living and facing death.

Lewis emphasizes that the one essential component for the cultivation and practice of all the virtues is that of courage – the willingness to face opposition, endure pain, and the resolute faith and conviction to follow through on what one knows to be True, Good, and Beautiful regardless of the consequences. It was in that context that Lewis wrote in his essay, "Is Progress Possible?"

> I care far more how humanity lives than how long. Progress, for me, means increasing goodness and happiness of individual lives. For [humanity], as for each man, mere longevity seems to me a contemptible ideal. [C. S. Lewis, "Is Progress Possible?" in Walter Hooper, ed., *God in the Dock: Essays on Theology and Ethics*, p. 311.]

Although Lewis focuses on perennial moral virtues and obligations, his arguments can be applied to a broad range of contemporary issues: everything from the exploitation of the environment to the modern education fad of "diversity", Big Brother-style government (under the guise of democratic socialism) that seeks to micro-manage the lives of its citizens, Artificial Intelligence, and the amoral use of biotechnology in fields such as genetic engineering, human cloning, and transhumanism.

In my book, *Natural Law: The Moral Foundation for Social and Political Civility* (2016), I trace the philosophical origins and development of Natural Law theory from the time of Socrates, Plato and Aristotle to the apostle Paul's utilization of the concept in his Epistle to the Romans, then subsequently in the writings of others including Augustine of Hippo, Thomas Aquinas, Martin Luther, John Calvin, William Blackstone, John Locke and Thomas Jefferson down to Robert Bork and Clarence Thomas in recent times. In summary, the following chart on page 12 highlights some of the defining principles of traditional Natural Law.

Natural Law theory is controversial because it presupposes that certain moral and ethical principles are absolute and universal, which in turn assumes the existence of a transcendent, eternal, and good God who is the divine Source of the moral law. Therefore, beginning in the second half of the Nineteenth Century legal scholars began arguing for an alternative theory known as Legal Positivism (or "Positive Law"). Rejecting the belief that law should be grounded on moral absolutes, Legal Positivists advocated a more pragmatic and relativistic theory of jurisprudence derived from social customs, common law, statutory and case law, and judicial precedent. By the turn of the Twentieth Century Positive Law was becoming the dominant philosophy in elite law schools in Great Britain and America so that by the 1940s traditional Natural Law was dismissed as a curious relic of the past. As Lewis argued in *The Abolition of Man*, the consequences of moral relativism would be catastrophic. We need only look at the moral disintegration in our society over the past sixty years as a prime example.

Some Basic Principles of Natural Law

There is a God (or gods, or "Fate", or some unifying power or principle) that is responsible for the existence and maintenance of the universe.

There is a moral law to which we are accountable. Certain attitudes, speech and actions are objectively right and wrong regardless of our personal/subjective feelings about them.

Standards of social decency and propriety.

The promotion of virtues such as wisdom, honor, courage, and moderation.

Honesty in normal interpersonal relations and commercial transactions.

The value of kindness, compassion, mercy, and forgiveness.

Respect for one's parents, elders, and ancestors.

Proper protection and provision for children.

Sexual restrictions: The sanctity of marriage, and prohibitions on sexual promiscuity, incest and rape.

The principle of reciprocity, and a tacit acknowledgment of the Golden Rule: "Do unto others as you would have them do unto you."

The rule of law (either a formal written code or informal customs.)

The sanctity of human life and a prohibition on murder.

The right of self-defense and protection from physical abuse by others.

Private property rights.

Protection from arbitrary government abuse or coercion.

Source: Jefrey D. Breshears, *Natural Law: The Moral Foundation for Social and Political Civility* (Centre•Pointe Publishing, 2016)

However, truth cannot be suppressed permanently, and occasionally these perennial principles reemerge in public discourse despite the efforts of secular humanistic cultural elites who deny their validity. Interestingly, this was a integral factor in the moral case for the modern civil rights movement in America in the 1950s and '60s. Martin Luther King Jr. often appealed to Natural Law to justify non-violent social protest, most notably in his famous "Letter from a Birmingham Jail." In response to his critics – in particular, local white ministers who criticized him for organizing unauthorized street demonstrations – King defended his actions on the basis of traditional Christian moral philosophy. In the following excerpt from his eloquent and erudite essay, he cited Augustine and Aquinas and drew a clear distinction between just and unjust laws derived from the precepts of Natural Law.

You express a great deal of anxiety over our willingness to break laws. This is certainly a legitimate concern. Since we so diligently urge people to obey the Supreme Court's decision of 1954 outlawing segregation in the public schools, it may seem rather paradoxical for us consciously to break laws.

One may ask: "How can you advocate breaking some laws and obeying others?" The answer lies in the fact that there are two types of laws: just and unjust. I would be the first to advocate obeying just laws. One has not only a legal but a moral responsibility to obey just laws. Conversely, one has a moral responsibility to disobey unjust laws. I would agree with St. Augustine that "an unjust law is no law at all."

Now, what is the difference between the two? How does one determine whether a law is just or unjust?

> A just law is a man-made code that squares with the moral law or the law of God. An unjust law is a code that is out of harmony with the moral law. To put it in the terms of St. Thomas Aquinas: An unjust law is a human law that is not rooted in eternal law and natural law. Any law that uplifts human personality is just. Any law that degrades human personality is unjust. All segregation statutes are unjust because segregation distorts the soul and damages the personality. It gives the segregator a false sense of superiority and the segregated a false sense of inferiority. [https://web.cn.edu/kwheeler/documents/Letter_Birmingham_Jail.pdf]

A Post-Script on Natural Law

Like many moral philosophers who preceded him, Lewis made a compelling case in defense of these universal moral and ethical standards based on Natural Law that are intrinsic to human nature. Nineteen hundred years earlier, the apostle Paul did the same in the first two chapters of his Epistle to the Romans:

> Rom. 1:18*ff* – For the wrath of God is being revealed from heaven against all the godlessness and wickedness of men who suppress the truth by their wickedness, since what may be known about God is plain to them, because God has made it plain to them. For since the creation of the world God's invisible qualities – his eternal power and divine nature – have been clearly seen, being understood from what has been made, so that men are without excuse.
>
> For although they knew God, they neither glorified him as God nor gave thanks to him, but their thinking became futile and their foolish hearts were darkened. Although they claimed to be wise, they became fools and exchanged the glory of the immortal God for [idols and] images....
>
> Therefore God gave them over in the sinful desires of their hearts to sexual impurity for the degrading of their bodies.... They exchanged the truth of God for a lie, and worshiped and served created things rather than the Creator.... Furthermore, since they did not think it worthwhile to retain the knowledge of God, he gave them over to a depraved mind....

> They have become filled with every kind of wickedness, evil, greed and depravity. They are full of envy, murder, strife, deceit and malice. They are gossips, slanderers, God-haters, insolent, arrogant and boastful, they invent ways of doing evil; they disobey their parents; they are senseless, faithless, heartless, ruthless. Although they know God's righteous decree that those who do such things deserve death, they not only continue to do these very things but also approve of those who practice them....
>
> Rom. 2:14ff – Indeed, when Gentiles, who do not have the [Mosaic] law, do by nature things required by the law, they are a law for themselves, even though they do not have the law, since they show that the requirements of the law are written on their hearts, their consciences also bearing witness, and their thoughts now accusing, now even defending them.

According to Paul, the solution to this moral dilemma is that one must be spiritually regenerated by the grace of God through faith in Jesus Christ and the indwelling presence of the Holy Spirit. Lewis likewise understood that humanity is fundamentally flawed by a sin nature and therefore incapable of fulfilling the requirements of God's moral standards. Furthermore, most people are not believers in Christ, in which case Natural Law functions as a baseline or a lowest-common-denominator for social decency and civility to which all citizens can be held accountable. Christians, however, are called to a much higher standard of moral and ethical behavior based on the teachings of the New Testament. Rather than a passive approach to others ("Do no harm"), Christians are commanded to proactively "Love others as you love yourself." But these higher values are for the community of Christians in society – those who voluntarily have surrendered their lives to Christ. As such, these values and practices exist outside the purview of government and cannot be imposed on others. Whenever Christians have attempted to do so in past centuries through the unholy alliance of church and state (the so-called age of "Christendom"), the result has been disastrous in terms of damaging the credibility as well as the moral authority of the church in society.

II. THE POLITICAL PHILOSOPHY OF C. S. LEWIS

An Aversion to Politics?

A common misconception is that C. S. Lewis had little if any interest in politics. Not only did Lewis' brother Warren ("Warnie") and several of his biographers perpetuate this idea, but Lewis himself often implied the same. For example, in a 1953 letter to Don Giovanni Calabria, Lewis declared that "above all other spheres of human life, the Devil claims politics for his own, as almost the citadel of his power," while in a 1958 letter to Mrs. Edward Allen he conceded that "Government is at its best a necessary evil."

According to Lewis' adopted stepson, Douglas Gresham, "Jack was not interested in politics" – a claim that biographer George Sayer affirms when he writes that Lewis "showed no interest whatsoever in politics." Furthermore, Warnie Lewis contended that his brother had "contempt for politics and politicians," and that this attitude extended back into their childhood as they were regularly subjected to a "torrent of [politically-charged] vituperation" on the part of their father and his associates. As Warnie recalled:

> Neighbors would from time to time drop in on an evening for a chat with our father, and in those days... amongst the upper middle class in Belfast, politics and money were almost the sole topics of conversation, with politics the main dish. At the best of times political conversation is of all conversation the dullest, and only bearable when two friends hold opposing political views. But such was not the case in any Belfast house I ever visited. The religious, political and social cleavage between the Protestant Unionist and the Roman Catholic Nationalist was as deep and rigid as that which separates the Moslem from the Hindu.... No man came to my father's house who did not hold exactly the same view as he did himself, [and it always

> became] a contest as to which could say the most insulting things about "this rotten Liberal Government".
> Consequently, we had to sit in silence whilst the torrent of vituperation flowed over our heads. The result in Jack's case was... to disgust him with the very word "politics" before he was out of his 'teens. [George Sayer, *Jack: A Life of C. S. Lewis*, p. 70.]

In fact, the truth of the matter is that Lewis was determinedly apolitical in the sense that he had no apparent interest in the machinations of politics – the "nuts-and-bolts" or "sausage-making" processes of government that involve covert deal-making in closed-door, smoke-filled rooms. To that end, Lewis avoided newspapers and the endless debates and public posturing regarding political policies. He fully understood that politics, including democratic politics, often attracts some of the most ambitious, power-hungry, unscrupulous and manipulative people in society. Such was his aversion to politicized ego-inflating showmanship that in 1951 he declined Prime Minister Winston Churchill's offer to bestow upon him the honorary title, "Commander of the Order of the British Empire," for his formidable literary accomplishments and inspiring radio addresses during World War II. Although he privately supported the Conservative Party by default, Lewis avoided any public association with a particular party or politician, nor did he donate money "to anything that had a directly political implication."

Temperamentally and intellectually, Lewis was unsuited for the rough-and-tumble mud-wrestling that is virtually a *de rigueur* component of democratic politics. As an influential Christian moral philosopher and theoretician, his was a higher calling. Lewis had a well-defined political philosophy, but it was macro-politics based on the universal principles of Natural Law that most concerned him – not the micro-politics that energizes and motivates most politicos. Paradoxically, it was precisely due to of his disinterest in micro-politics that Lewis was able to conceptualize and articulate with such profundity that which matters most: the proper role and scope of government.

Forays Into Political Thought

Beginning in his mid-twenties and in the wake of his service in World War I, Lewis expressed a distinct dislike for big government socialism. In his epic poem, "Dymer" (1926), he describes life in the "Perfect City", a pseudo-utopian society in which everyone's schedule is meticulously controlled by the state. Not only does the government determine one's vocation, income and living arrangement, but even when, where, and with whom one is allowed to have sexual contact. Lewis was not yet a Christian when he wrote the poem, but he regarded this kind of political control to be contrary to "Nature" and therefore immoral. The hero of the story, Dymer, rebels against the repressive authoritarianism of this fascist/socialist regime.

Following his conversion to Christianity in 1931, one of Lewis' main literary interests turned to Christian apologetics – explaining and defending the unique truth-claims of the Christian faith. Lewis understood Christianity to be not only a religion and a spiritual relationship with God, but also a comprehensive worldview that encompasses the whole of reality, including one's citizenship rights and responsibilities. Therefore, he was compelled to apply Christian principles to the morally-murky world of politics. Although, as previously discussed, he found the process of democratic politics to be repellant, he nonetheless developed a philosophy of government that was as rational, ethical and realistic as possible in such a sin-soaked and dysfunctional world. Over the next 25 years he wrote several works in which he expressed aspects of his political views, including:

- "On Bolshevism" (1939)
- "Why I Am Not a Pacifist" (1939)
- *The Abolition of Man* (1944)

- *Mere Christianity* – Book III, Chapter 3 on "Social Morality" (1944)
- "Bulverism: The Foundation of 20th Century Thought" (1944)
- *That Hideous Strength* – Book III in the Space Trilogy (1945)
- "Membership" (1945)
- "A Reply to Professor Haldane" (1956)
- "Is Progress Possible? Willing Slaves of the Welfare State" (1958)
- "Screwtape Proposes a Toast" (1959 – an epilogue to *The Screwtape Letters*

In addition to Lewis' own writings, three other works in particular shed valuable insight into his political philosophy:
- John G. West, "Finding the Permanent in the Political: C. S. Lewis as a Political Thinker"
- Gilbert Meilander, *The Taste for the Other: The Social and Ethical Thought of C. S. Lewis* (1978)
- Justin Buckley Dyer and Micah J. Watson, *C. S. Lewis on Politics and the Natural Law* (2016)

Regarding politics and government, Lewis was the consummate realist who was neither ignorant nor naive regarding political history and philosophy. According to the renowned Oxford historian, A. J. P. Taylor, Lewis "helped in the history school [at Magdalen College] by teaching political theory," and in 1939 he wrote an essay entitled "On Bolshevism" in which he essentially identified Soviet Communism as Nazism's evil twin. As noted earlier, Lewis was one of relatively few faculty members at Oxford who understood the diabolical nature of Marxism, and in his 1944 essay, "Bulverism: The Foundation of Twentieth Century Thought," he attributed the general breakdown in private and public morality to two insidious influences: Freudianism and Marxism. (In later writings he would also include Darwinism in the mix.) Regarding Marxism in particular, he focused on the simplistic sociological stereotyping that characterized Marx's theory of history: the perpetual class struggle between the rich and the poor (or in

Nineteenth Century terms, the bourgeoisie versus the proletariat). Such a philosophy is deterministic and presupposes that human beings are merely the hapless products of the economic forces that impact their lives. Lewis regarded such a generalization to be essentially dehumanizing in the sense that it robs human beings of their innate and unique individuality. Beyond that, it is also illogical, as he explained in his essay on "Bulverism."

> The Marxist will tell you to go and examine the economic interests of the hundred; you will find that they all think freedom a good thing because they are all members of the bourgeoisie, whose prosperity is increased by a policy of *laissez-faire* [i.e., free enterprise capitalism]. Their thoughts are 'Ideologically tainted' at the source....
>
> There are two questions that people who say this kind of things ought to be asked. The first is, "Are *all* thoughts thus tainted at the source, or only some?" The second is, "Does the taint invalidate the tainted thought – in the sense of making it untrue – or not?"
>
> If they say that *all thoughts* are thus tainted, then, of course, we must remind them that Freudianism and Marxism are as much systems of thought as Christian theology or philosophical idealism. The Freudian and the Marxian are in the same boat with the rest of us, and cannot criticize us from outside. They have sawn off the branch they were sitting on. If, on the other hand, they say that the taint need not invalidate their thinking, then neither need it invalidate ours. In which case they have saved their own branch, but also saved ours along with it. ["Bulverism," in Walter Hooper, ed., *C. S. Lewis: God in the Dock*, p. 271.]

Lewis referred to this kind of simplistic determinism as "Bulverism," and he concluded by observing:

> I see Bulverism at work in every political argument. The capitalists must be bad economists because we know why they want capitalism [i.e., they profit from it], and equally the Communists must be bad economists

> because we know why they want Communism [i.e., they want to overthrow the bourgeoisie by violent revolution and become the new ruling class].... In reality, of course, either the doctrines of the capitalists are false, or the doctrines of the Communists, or both; but you can only find out the rights and wrongs by [facts and] reasoning – never by being rude about your opponent's psychology. [Ibid., p. 274]

In other words, according to Lewis, arguments should be won or lost on the bases of facts and sound reasoning rather than amateurish psychoanalysis. We must show *that* a person is wrong before trying to explain *why* the person is wrong. We don't defend our beliefs and critique those of others based on some pretense of knowing their motives. Nor can we defend our beliefs and defeat those of others on the bases of their group identify – be it their socio-economic status, their race, sex, ethnicity, religion, or their occupation. As Lewis warns, "Until Bulverism is crushed, reason can play no effective part in human affairs."

In conjunction with Freudian psychoanalysis, Marxism is a deterministic and dehumanizing ideology. This mentality is also, of course, the philosophical basis for the contemporary Neo-Marxist pathological obsession with group identity.

As a first-rate thinker with an exceptional education and a strong moral conscience, Lewis was eminently qualified to write and teach on political issues – a key point that Justin Buckley Dyer and Micah J. Watson emphasize in their insightful book, *C. S. Lewis on Politics and the Natural Law*:

> With an education hard to imagine today, Lewis could appreciate the intellectual and philosophical transitions that had transpired from Plato to [John] Locke to the contemporary theorists of his own day.... With his background in the ancient Greeks as well as the Scholastics and early modern thinkers, Lewis was well versed in philosophy and ethics and political thought, including natural law theory. [Justin Buckley Dyer and Micah J. Watson, *C. S. Lewis on Politics and the Natural Law*, p. 10]

Politically astute, Lewis did not devalue the importance of government. It is, as he was prone to note, "a necessary evil" given the realities of human nature. Although all manmade systems and institutions are flawed and corrupt in various degrees, some are obviously better than others. Only a fool would fail to see a qualitative difference between Great Britain's Parliamentary government or the system that America's Founding Fathers established and that of Nazi Germany, Communist China, or any Islamic state. Furthermore, only in a dysfunctional and/or despotic political system must common people constantly worry about natural rights and laws. In a normal (i.e., "good") society, people would mind their own business and go about their daily lives with relatively little concern about how the government is operating, as Lewis noted in his essay, "Membership," written in 1945:

> But do not let us mistake necessary evils for good.... A sick society must think much about politics, as a sick man must think much about his digestion: to ignore the subject may be fatal cowardice for the one as for the other. But if either comes to regard it as the natural food of the mind – if either forgets that we think of such things only in order to be able to think of something else – then what was undertaken for the sake of health has become itself a new and deadly disease. [C. S. Lewis, "Membership." Cited in Walter Hooper, ed., *The Weight of Glory and Other Addresses*, p. 162.]

A Rational, Ethical and Realistic Political Philosophy

C. S. Lewis defied strict political categorization, and he generally resisted being identified with any particular socio/political ideology. In *Mere Christianity* he wrote that the Christian faith should not be tied to any specific political program, and a truly Christian view of society and politics would conform neither to standard conservative nor left-wing thinking. Although generally a traditionalist, he was not necessarily a conservative in the conventional sense. He adamantly disapproved of the traditional elitist class system in Britain, and he rejected the idea that the primary measure of a good society is necessarily its material prosperity and standard of living. Based on a realistic understanding of human nature, he certainly was no libertarian. He valued morality and nature over unrestrained freedom, economic development, and science and technology. He was also not a small 'd' democrat. For good reasons, he distrusted the common man [and woman] to be wise and just. But neither was Lewis a Christian socialist. No simpleton, he was equally convinced that both capitalists and socialists have an inherent sin problem. However, so far as is known, he never voted for the socialist British Labour Party.

In effect, Lewis understood the civic role of the thoughtful Christian to be analogous to that of a "watchman" who offers a biblically-based prophetic critique of contemporary society and culture in keeping with theme of Isaiah 21:6*ff*:

This is what the Lord says to me:
"Go, post a watchman and have him report what he sees...
Let him be fully alert...."
Day after day, my lord, I stand on the watchtower;
Every night I stay at my post.

In light of that perceived calling, Lewis adopted a political philosophy that was rational, ethical and realistic based primarily on two major influences.

(1) Natural Law ethics. As discussed earlier, Lewis believed in objective moral and ethical realities, discernible as a result of our having been created in the image of God with a rational mind and a moral conscience in keeping with the apostle Paul's statements in his Epistle to the Romans (see page 14). These universal moral truths are an integral aspect of general revelation and therefore applicable to normal human relations. Otherwise, there would be no common ground on which Christians and non-Christians could meet to debate and negotiate public policies. In that regard, all "just" laws and all prudent social and political policies are expressions of the Natural Law – as Martin Luther King Jr. so eloquently emphasized in his aforementioned "Letter from a Birmingham Jail."

(2) Classical Liberal ideology. John Locke (1632-1704), regarded by many as the most brilliant and influential political theorist of the Enlightenment era, formalized the basic principles of what is known as Classical Liberalism (not to be confused with modern liberalism). Locke's political philosophy set forth many of the foundational concepts later incorporated into the American Declaration of Independence and the U.S. Constitution, including fundamental principles such as:

- The natural ("inalienable") rights of all citizens.
- The social contract theory of government in which legitimate political institutions exist by the consent of the governed.
- Representative republican-style government – but not a democracy (see below).
- Constitutional government and the rule of law.
- Limited government based on the principle: "That government is best which governs least."

The essence of Locke's political philosophy is the principle that legitimate government exists to serve the interests of its citizens rather than vice-versa. More specifically, government is instituted to defend its citizens and protect their basic right to life, liberty, and property (including their own selves). As Lewis summarized the role of government in *Mere Christianity*, politics should function as the means by which government facilitates human flourishing. In his words, "The State exists simply to promote and to protect the ordinary happiness of human beings in this life." In that regard, Lewis was fundamentally a classical liberal. However, he was not a *laissez-faire* conservative nor a libertarian in that he valued morality, tradition, true social justice, and nature over the pursuit of individual wealth and unrestrained development, science and technology. In keeping with a basic tenet of Natural Law, he believed the common good should prevail over libertarian individualism (ref. page 12).

On Democracy

As one would expect, Lewis' political philosophy derived from his understanding of human nature. Lewis was no Calvinist, but in this regard he would have agreed with John Calvin that the basis for any proper relationship between citizens and their government is a sober and realistic awareness of human nature, or as Calvin put it: "Wisdom lies in knowing God and knowing oneself." According to Scripture, human beings are self-centered egoists who need well-defined boundaries for appropriate behavior. Therefore, government is an absolutely necessary institution. In Federalist No. 51 James Madison stated the issue this way: "If men were angels, no government would be necessary."

However... there is a complicating factor: Government itself is staffed by sinful human beings, so its powers must be limited and carefully controlled. Again, Madison proposed a realistic solution to the problem. In the same essay, Federalist No. 51, he noted: "In framing a government, which is to be administered by men over men, the great difficulty lies in this: you must first enable the government to control the governed; and in the next place oblige it to control itself." As the American statesman and Presbyterian minister John Witherspoon explained at the time, "Every good form of government must be complex... so that one may check the other." This was the "separation of powers" concept popularized by the Enlightenment French philosopher, Baron de Montesquieu, who argued in *The Spirit of the Laws* (1748) that "power checks power."

In *Mere Christianity* Lewis summarized what he regarded as "the key to history." Just as every human being has a life cycle, so do human institutions and civilizations. Terrific energy is spent building these institutions and civilizations over generations, only to have it all ruined by the egoism, pride, and greed of man. Sooner or later, the most selfish, ambitious and cruel people claw their way to the top and bring on misery and ruin.

Eventually, the lust for power corrupts most of the good that institutions and civilizations are founded upon, including those established on enlightened principles of "life, liberty, and the pursuit of happiness." Therefore, liberty must be balanced by private and public virtue in keeping with Natural Law principles. As Lewis noted in *Mere Christianity*, "You cannot make men good by law; and without good men you cannot have a good society. That is why we must go on to think... of morality inside the individual." America's Founding Fathers understood this principle well and often commented on it:

- John Adams: "We have no government armed with powers capable of contending with human passions unbridled by morality and religion.... Our Constitution was made only for a moral and religious people. It is wholly inadequate to govern any other."
- John Adams: "Public virtue cannot exist without private, and public virtue is the only foundation of Republics."
- Benjamin Franklin: "Only a virtuous people are capable of freedom."
- George Washington: "The foundations of our National policy will be laid in the pure and immutable principles of private morality."
- James Madison: "We have staked the whole of all our political institutions upon the capacity of mankind for self-government, upon the capacity of each and all of us to govern

ourselves, to control ourselves, to sustain ourselves according to the Ten Commandments of God."

C. S. Lewis detested the traditional elitist and hierarchical class system of England, but he also had little confidence in democracy. Lewis understood that most people are poorly educated, small-minded, selfish, and neither wise nor discerning. Undoubtedly, he would have agreed with Winston Churchill's comment that "the best argument against democracy is a five-minute conversation with the average citizen." Therefore, according to Lewis, "the real reason for democracy" is not that most people are wise and good, but just the reverse: "Mankind is so fallen that no man can be trusted with unchecked power over his fellows."*

In his 1945 essay,"Membership," Lewis expressed an uneasy ambivalence toward democracy. While he believed in political equality under the law, he was quick to point out that there were two "opposite reasons" for being a democrat. First: "You may think all men so good that they deserve a share in the government of the commonwealth, and so wise that the commonwealth needs their advice" – a view that he rejected as "a false, romantic doctrine of democracy." Conversely, however, "democracy is rooted in the reality that everyone is morally flawed, and therefore some form of representative government is necessary because [to cite Lord Acton] 'power corrupts, and absolute power corrupts absolutely.'"**

Lewis challenged the fundamental assumption of democratic egalitarianism – the fantasy that all people are in fact "equal"– as demonstrably absurd. In a 1959 letter to an American newspaper editor, Dan Tucker, Lewis argued that democracy, in conjunction with the mainstream media and a mediocre education system, assures that the general public remains comfortably pacified, docile, and easily manipulated by the governing class.

---

* Cited in Justin Buckley Dyer and Micah J. Watson, *C. S. Lewis on Politics and the Natural Law*, p. 98.

** C. S. Lewis, "Membership," in *The Weight of Glory and Other Addresses*, p. 168.

> A hundred years ago we all thought that Democracy was it. Neither you nor I probably think so now. It neither allows the ordinary man to control legislation nor qualifies him to do so. The real questions are settled in secret and the newspapers keep us occupied with [mostly trivial] issues. And this is all the easier because democracy always in the end destroys education. [Cited in Justin Buckley Dyer and Micah J. Watson, *C. S. Lewis on Politics and the Natural Law*, p. 6.]

About the same time, Lewis wrote an incisive critique of democracy in an epilogue to *The Screwtape Letters* entitled "Screwtape Proposes a Toast" (1959) in which he reiterated his belief that democracy is a lowest-common-denominator political system that rewards mediocrity and social conformity. In fact, he charged, "Democracy does not want great men," and he proceeded to explain what he regarded as the fundamental flaw in the democratic ideal. Assuming the persona of a senior demon intent on wreaking havoc in Western civilization, he delivers this chilling instruction to his eager minions:

> Democracy is the word with which you must lead [the masses] by the nose....
> You are to use the word purely as an incantation.... It is a name they venerate. And of course it is connected with the political ideal that men should be equally treated. You then make a stealthy transition in their minds from this political ideal to a factual belief that all men *are* equal....
> Under the influence of this incantation those who are in any or every way inferior can labour more wholeheartedly and successfully than ever before to pull down everyone else to their own level.
> What I want to fix your attention on is the vast, overall movement towards the discrediting, and finally the elimination, of every kind of human excellence – moral, cultural, social, or intellectual. [C. S. Lewis, *The Screwtape Letters*, pp. 205, 97*ff*.]

Speaking through Screwtape, Lewis reiterates a common mantra and the central theme of democratic mythology: Every individual is equal – not just in terms of equitable treatment under the law, but equal in reality! As Americans have witnessed in recent decades, this illusion has a devastating affect on state-controlled public (and often private) education in terms of dumbing-down the curriculum, lowering standards, inflating grades, coddling students, and promoting the cult of "self-esteem". As Lewis puts it, "The teachers – or should I say, nurses? – will be far too busy reassuring the dunces and patting them on the back to waste any time on real teaching," and concludes with this prophetic warning so characteristic of our day:

> Democracy... leads to a nation without great men, a nation mainly of subliterates, morally [weak] from lack of discipline in youth, full of the cocksureness which flattery breeds on ignorance, and soft from lifelong pampering. And that of course is what Hell wishes every democratic people to be. [Ibid., p. 201*ff*]

Given Lewis' contempt for classical conservatism (founded on the wobbly tripod of hereditary monarchy, a rigidly hierarchical class system and an official state church) and his pessimism regarding modern democracy, what kind of political system would he have preferred? Most likely, he would have opted for the kind of constitutional republic on which America was originally founded: one in which a written covenant such as the U.S. Constitution was derived from the unwritten covenant of Natural Law. While being prudently democratic, republicanism set reasonable qualifications for participatory citizenship. While acknowledging that all citizens are entitled to fundamental human rights and equal justice under the law, it also recognized that the right to vote is not an entitlement. Some lack the basic cultural literacy and education to understand how a republican-style system should operate, while others disqualify themselves on the basis of poor character (convicted felons, for example). In addition, there are those who cannot be trusted to vote responsibly and in the public interest because they are perpetual welfare recipients who will naturally support politicians who promise them the most benefits from the public treasury.

Unfortunately, republican-style government discredited itself in American history almost from the outset due to its exclusion of all women and non-whites. In addition, only property owners were eligible to vote and serve in public office on the assumption that they alone had a vested interest and sufficient stake in the system and would therefore be less susceptible to radical propaganda and anarchist tendencies. While the wholesale exclusion of women and non-whites was unjustifiable and inexcusable, and extending voting rights exclusively to property holders was questionable at best, certainly a case can be made for denying the voting franchise to convicted felons, those who lack fluency in the English language, and those who receive a substantial portion of their income from taxpayer-funded public welfare programs. (Reasonable exceptions, of course, can be granted to disabled individuals and victims of unusual circumstances.) Furthermore, voter-registration laws that require proof of citizenship and photo I.D.'s should be mandatory so as to minimize voting fraud and assure election integrity.

Like America's Founding Fathers, C. S. Lewis understood that democracies tend to have relatively short life cycles as a matter of course. Historically, democracies always degenerate through a process of general moral decline, internal corruption and poor leadership as more and more citizens abandon the higher principles of Natural Law in favor of electing officials who pander to their whims. This view of history, commonly associated with the Scottish historian Alexander Fraser Tytler (1747-1813) and often referred to as the "Tytler Cycle of History," is summarized as follows:

> A democracy is always temporary in nature; it simply cannot exist as a permanent form of government. A democracy will continue to exist up until the time that voters discover that they can vote themselves generous gifts from the public treasury. From that moment on, the majority always votes for the

candidates who promise the most benefits from the public treasury, with the result that every democracy will finally collapse due to loose fiscal policy, which is always followed by a dictatorship. [https://en.wikipedia.org/wiki/Alexander_Fraser_Tytler,_Lord_Woodhouselee]

According to this theory, the average age of the world's greatest civilizations from the beginning of recorded history is about 200 years. During those two centuries, these nations typically progressed and then regressed through the following sequence:

- From bondage to spiritual faith.
- From spiritual faith to great courage.
- From courage to liberty.
- From liberty to abundance.
- From abundance to selfishness.
- From selfishness to complacency.
- From complacency to apathy.
- From apathy to dependence.
- From dependence back into bondage.

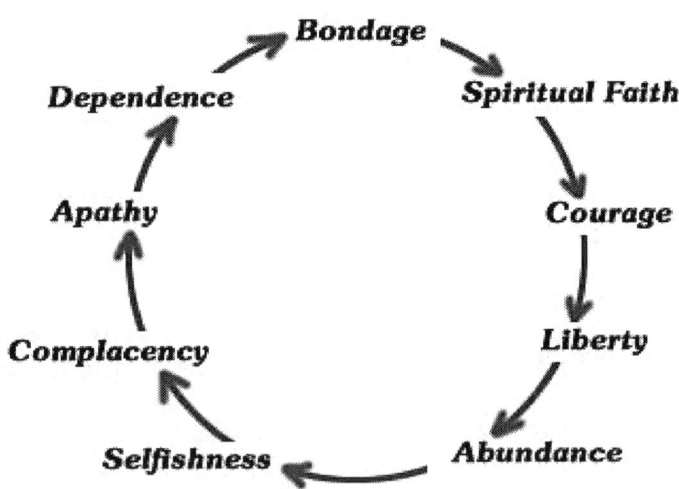

The Tytler Cycle of History

Two Threats to Western Civilization

In his political writings, Lewis tended to focus on what he regarded at the time as the two most ominous threats facing Western civilization:

(1) "Technocracy"– A scientific- and technological-industrial complex driven by amoral secular humanistic values. As Jacques Ellul would later argue in *The Technological Society* (1954), there must be moral and ethical limits on the development and utilization of science and technology. Ellul (1912-94), a French philosopher, sociologist, and (unorthodox) Christian, was convinced that the cult of technology posed the greatest threat to human freedom and  religious values. In the modern technological society dominated by transnational corporations, what matters most is that something is newer, faster, more powerful, and more efficient – with no regard as to its spiritual, mental or moral effects. For scientists, technocrats, corporate executives and the majority of stockholders, the questions are always, "Can we do this?" and "How profitable will it be?" rather than "Should we do this?" or "What will be the future effects of it?" Free enterprise and unregulated science and technology, which began innocuously as a servant of humankind and a means to an end, has become an autonomous force that threatens to dominate our lives.

Lewis would essentially agree. Influenced in part by G. K. Chesterton's *Eugenics and Other Evils: An Argument Against the Scientifically Organized State* (1922), Lewis was convinced that an unholy alliance of scientism (promoted through the secular religion of atheistic naturalism and Darwinian evolutionary theory) and Enlightenment Rationalism have undermined traditional Christian values by sacralizing economic production and corporate profits.

Competing economic systems, whether capitalist, socialist or communist, all share at least one thing in common: they are essentially materialistic and amoral.* According to Lewis (and Ellul), the competition for technological dominance is a major factor in the growth of political centralization and authoritarianism even in democratic nations.

[Note: In contemporary terms, one can readily see the effects of this profit-driven corporate capitalistic technocracy and its insatiable obsession in penetrating global markets regardless of any social, political or moral consequences. Consider the amoral and soulless marketing strategies of multinational corporations such as Microsoft, Apple, Google, Facebook, Nike, etc. – and even sports mega-corporations such as the National Basketball Association.]

As is obvious in several of his writings, particularly his "Space Trilogy," Lewis was generally unimpressed by the exalted status accorded scientists – especially those who utilized their genius for the purpose of exerting power over humankind. (Consider the theme of J. R. R. Tolkien's *The Lord of the Rings*.) In his essay, "Finding the Permanent in the Political: C. S. Lewis as a Political Thinker," John G. West notes Lewis' skepticism regarding the moral wisdom of most physical scientists, few of whom have been trained in moral philosophy (or political philosophy). As West explains:

> As for the objection that we must rely on the advice of scientists, because only they have the answers to today's complicated problems, Lewis could not agree. Lewis does not dispute that scientists have plenty of knowledge; the problem is that most of it is irrelevant [to the great moral, political, and transcendent issues of the day]. Political problems are preeminently moral problems, and scientists are not equipped to function as moralists. Said Lewis, "I dread specialists in power

---

* This should not be interpreted as implying that capitalism and socialism are functionally equivalent. The fundamental purpose of an economic system is the generation of wealth via the production of goods and services, and by that standard free enterprise capitalism out-performs any socialist system by far.

because they are specialists speaking outside their special subjects. Let scientists tell us about sciences. But government involves questions about the good for man, and justice, and what things are worth having at what price; and on these a scientific training gives a man's opinion no added value." [John G. West, "Finding the Permanent in the Political: C. S. Lewis as a Political Thinker." https://www.discovery.org/a/457/#]

West contends that science adds little value to political philosophy because it is "divorced from those permanent principles of morality upon which all just political solutions depend." Concepts such as justice, ethics and morality are "terms without meaning within the scientific framework." As a result, "[science] can easily become a tool for tyrants because it has no firm grounding in morality."

(2) The emergence of a "World Welfare State" – a socialistic "New World Order" rooted in secular humanistic philosophical values. In this new global society, the government conditions, regulates and controls the lives of its citizens as they grow increasingly dependent upon the state for their basic needs and desires. In the generation following Lewis' death in 1963, the European Common Market was transformed into the European Union with the stated objective to eliminate not only national boundaries but national distinctives, resulting in open borders and open immigration in Europe and eventually in the United States.

III. RUMINATIONS ON 'THE GOOD SOCIETY'

Conservatism, Socialism, and the Modern Welfare State

For better or for worse, a society and its culture play a crucial role in the cultivation of the moral consciousness of its citizens. Human beings are social creatures, and all are to some degree or another products of their nature, their nurture, and the *Zeitgeist* of their times. Although our society and culture do not determine who and what we are in the sense that we always retain some degree of free will and self-determination, they nonetheless condition (or influence) our sensibilities, as Gilbert Meilander notes in *The Taste of the Other: The Social and Ethical Thought of C. S. Lewis*:

> The pursuit of the moral life is not an isolated pursuit. Lewis, like Aristotle, believes that moral principles are learned indirectly from others around us, who serve as exemplars. And he, again like Aristotle, suggests that it will be extremely difficult to develop virtuous individuals apart from a virtuous society. [Gilbert Meilander, *The Taste for the Other: The Social and Ethical Thought of C. S. Lewis*, p. 212.]

In *Mere Christianity* (Book III, Chapter 3: "Social Morality"), Lewis sets forth some common sense guidelines for a "good" and just society and government based on the principles of Natural Law. The intent of the chapter is to demonstrate how generic Natural Law concepts, consistent with Christian values, would influence and regulate the social and political systems in a relatively harmonious, well-functioning and healthy society.

Regarding the Bible and government, Lewis understood the temptation for political power that appeals to many Christians, often for admirable reasons. However, both theology and history argue the contrary. The kind of sacralistic union of church and state that dominated Western "Christendom" for some 1400 years was not only counter-productive but largely discredited genuine Christian faith. Lewis rejected this tradition of Christian sacralism and the unholy alliance of church and state. Nothing could be more antithetical to the true spirit of the Gospel than compulsory and coercive state religion. Therefore, although aware that the Bible sanctions certain principles and goals for political ends, Lewis nevertheless acknowledged that Scripture does not provide specific guidance for political means to those ends. Given the radically different culture in which the New Testament was written, Christians should not expect it to offer, in his words, "a detailed political programme" for governing any modern society.

According to Lewis, good government operates according to the principles of Natural Law for the well-being of all, but it shouldn't be expected to enforce specifically Christian moral and ethical standards. In a 1945 essay entitled "Christian Apologetics," Lewis noted the proper relationship between biblical theology and politics:

> Theology teaches us what ends are desirable and what means are lawful, while Politics teaches what means can be effective. Thus Theology tells us that every man ought to have a decent wage. Politics tells by what means this is likely to be attained. Theology tells us which of these means are consistent with justice and charity. On the political question guidance comes not from Revelation but from natural prudence, knowledge of complicated facts and ripe experience.
> [C. S. Lewis, "Christian Apologetics," in Walter Hooper, ed., *God in the Dock*, p. 94.]

Lewis was careful to distinguish between his concept of a Good Society and a theocratic state such as Old Testament Israel. Ancient Israel was a unique nation in all of history, and its laws (civil, ceremonial, and even some moral laws) are not applicable to secular states. On this point, Lewis was quite emphatic, even to the point of referring to theocracy as "the worst of all [possible] governments."

> I believe that no man or group of men is good enough to be trusted with uncontrolled power over others. And the higher the pretensions of such power, the more dangerous.... Hence Theocracy is the worst of all governments. [C. S. Lewis, "A Reply to Professor Haldane" (1956), in *Of Other Worlds: Essays and Stories*, p. 81.]

Therefore, a Good Society would not be a theocratic or sacralistic system, nor should Christians attempt to impose specifically biblical standards of personal morality on mainstream society. Such an effort, as well-meaning as it may be, works only to damage the credibility of the Christian faith. As John West notes in "Finding the Permanent in the Political: C. S. Lewis as a Political Thinker," the Bible is not a textbook on political science, nor does it provide "particular advice on specific political issues." Furthermore, "in a society that is not a theocracy the Bible can never be the only standard of morality." This is why America's Founding Fathers, including the orthodox Christians among them, spoke and wrote of the "Laws of Nature and Nature's God." For them, Natural Law functioned as the essential common ground for all citizens regardless of their religious convictions.

There are, of course, complex and complicating factors in any attempt to govern a diverse (and predominantly secular) society. This was the context in which Lewis wrote that personal sins should only be treated as crimes to the extent that they cause demonstrable harm to another person or persons (including the most innocent of victims: pre-born babies). That being the case, Lewis concedes that most behavior between consenting adults should be tolerated – but certainly not officially sanctioned or promoted. This raises serious questions regarding issues such as prostitution, pornography, and the legalization of highly-addictive drugs.]

Likewise – and contrary to the presumptions and agendas of many contemporary "social justice" Christians – New Testament social and economic values cannot be imposed on mainstream society. Biblical moral, social, and economic values are for the voluntary society of the church. Mainstream society is not, and never will be, authentically Christian. Obviously, every society would be far better if more people lived by biblical standards, but there are reasonable limits to which we can mandate that non-Christians abide by specifically Christian values, including those related to charitable benevolence. Undoubtedly, Lewis would have condemned the agenda of contemporary "social justice" Christians. Like Fundamentalists in the past who attempted to control the private lives of Christians and non-Christians alike, liberal and left-wing Christians today support a big government agenda designed to forcibly regulate the public lives of citizens. Lewis would have regarded such laws and policies to be more Marxist than Christian.

Conversely, a Good Society, while tolerating and protecting individual freedom within all properly broad parameters, would not promote blatant immorality or irresponsible behavior and lifestyles. Instead, government, churches and other social institutions would strive to cultivate harmony between individuals in keeping with the "Golden Rule" ("Do unto others as you would have them do unto you") and on the basis of the traditional "Cardinal Virtues" (Prudence, temperance, justice, and fortitude). Given the realities of human nature, however, and the extent to which citizens in free societies often use their rights irresponsibly, the kind of Good Society such as Lewis envisioned seems hopelessly utopian. Nonetheless, he sets forth admirable goals. Whether attainable or not, they at least constitute principles on which Christians can live so as carry out their mandate to be a source of Light and Truth.

In *Mere Christianity* Lewis contends that in many respects a Good Society would be "conservative" – one that honors certain traditional values including:
- The basic principles of Natural Law and classical liberal political ideology.
- Traditional morals and manners such as honesty, decency, and civility.
- Traditional family values.
- Respect for one's elders.
- Respect for authority in general.
- Traditional sexual moral standards.

While providing for those who are legitimate victims of misfortune, a Good Society would encourage and require individual responsibility and discourage dependency. A Good Society would extend help to those in need while correspondingly holding them accountable to improve their life condition. In general, this would entail some form of workfare rather than entitlement-based welfare for the unemployed. In keeping with the apostle Paul's emphatic admonition in II Thess. 3:10 – "If a man does not work, he ought not to eat" – Lewis states that in a Good Society there would be "No passengers and no parasites" who seek to exploit the working classes in society.

[Note: Social welfare programs should always be administered as temporary means to help citizens in unusual situations who truly are victims of misfortune. Until the late 1960s, even most liberal Democrats agreed that welfare should never become a lifestyle. In 1935 President Franklin D. Roosevelt declared, "The federal government should, and will, get out of this business of relief. To dole out welfare is to administer a narcotic, a subtle destroyer of the human will." In that regard, he was indisputably correct. But by the late Sixties, with the expansion of Lyndon Johnson's "Great Society" welfare state, public assistance was redefined by liberals as a basic "right." As Alexander Tytler had predicted more than a century and a half earlier, politicians realized they could buy the support of an ever-growing bloc of voters by turning public assistance into welfare entitlements.]

Furthermore, a Good Society would respect and honor "Good Work" – or as Lewis put it, "[E]very one's work [should be] to produce something good" – i.e., something of true value. He proceeded to explain: "[T]here would be no manufacture of silly luxuries and then of sillier advertisements to persuade us to buy them." In this regard, Lewis likely would have endorsed the British economist E. F. Schumacher's moral philosophy of employment set forth in his book, *Good Work* (1979), in which Schumacher challenged his readers to carefully consider the intrinsic value of their chosen vocation:

Considering the centrality of work in human life, one might have expected that every textbook on economics, sociology, politics, and related subjects would present a theory of work as one of the indispensable foundation stones for all further expositions. After all, it is work which occupies most of the energies of the human race,  and what people actually *do* is normally more important for understanding them than what they say, or what they spend their money on, or what they own, or how they vote. A person's work is undoubtedly one of the most decisive formative influences on his character and personality.... [But] the question of what the work does to the worker is hardly ever asked.

From this, I derive the three purposes of human work as follows:

First, to provide necessary and useful goods and services.

Second, to enable every one of us to use and thereby perfect our gifts like good stewards.

Third, to do so in service to, and in cooperation with, others, so as to liberate ourselves from our inborn egocentrism. [E. F. Schumacher, *Good Work*, p. 3.]

Paradoxically – and ironically, given his antipathy for left-wing authoritarianism – Lewis also believed that in some respects a Good Society would be in a sense "socialistic". This was, perhaps an unfortunate choice of words, although it was regarded as a perfectly respectable political philosophy in Britain (and to a lesser extent, in America) at the time. Clearly, what Lewis had in mind was a society based on cooperation rather than ruthless and predatory competition. In that regard it would be a charitable society that promotes the common good over purely individualistic rights.* Perhaps most

---

* See Jefrey D. Breshears, *Natural Law: The Moral Foundation for Social and Political Civility*, pp. 16-19.

radically, Lewis argues that a Good Society would also reject a fundamental component of capitalism: usury, or lending money at interest. He cites three great civilizations – the Greeks, the Hebrews, and medieval Christendom – all of which condemned "the very thing on which we base our whole [economic] life" – i.e., the modern banking system.

Interestingly, in the epilogue of *The Screwtape Letters* entitled "Screwtape Proposes a Toast" (1959), Lewis writes that Nineteenth Century Christian socialism posed the greatest threat to the kingdom of darkness in this world.* Classism has always been a source of injustice, exploitation, tension and conflict in history, and Christian-based social ethics offers the only realistic alternative to this ongoing problem. Far more than just utopian democratic socialists, many astute political observers over the past 250 years have warned of the dangers of class divisions in society:

- John Adams: "In every society where property exists there will ever be a struggle between rich and poor."
- James Madison in the Federalist No. 10: "The most common... source of [conflict] has been the various and unequal distribution of property."
- The Working Men's Republican Political Association (1835): "There appear to exist two distinct classes, the rich and the poor; the oppressed and the oppressor; those that live by their own labor and they that live by the labor of others; the

---

* It should be emphasized that "socialism" is an expansive term that covers a wide range of social, economic and political orientations and policies. As commonly used, socialism refers to everything from relatively moderate "reformist" socialism characterized by the British Labour Party, the Democratic Party in America, and modern European welfare states to radical "revolutionary" socialistic states such as the totalitarian Marxist/ Communist regimes of China, North Korea, Cuba, and the former Soviet Union. That being the case, the socialist spectrum is more of a sliding-scale continuum than one delineated by a fixed position. Lewis' use of the term drew a distinction between 19th Century-style democratic socialism, influenced in part by Christian humanitarian impulses, and secular/totalitarian Marxism based on violent revolution, the abolition of capitalism and private property, and the elimination of basic human rights.

aristocratic and the democratic; the despotic and the republican, who are in direct opposition to one another in their objects and pursuits."
- The Populist Manifesto (1892): "On the one side are the allied hosts of the monopolies, the money power, great trusts and railroad corporations, who seek the enactment of laws to benefit them and impoverish the people; on the other are the farmers, laborers, merchants, and all other people who produce wealth and bear the burdens of taxation...."
- Helen Keller (1911): "This country is governed for the richest, for the corporations, the bankers, the land speculators, and for the exploiters of labor."

Significantly, voluntary "socialism" was a prominent distinguishing feature of Christian social ethics as practiced in the early church and promoted by the apostle Paul, as several New Testament passages relate:

- Regarding the early church in Jerusalem, we read in Acts 2:42-45 that the followers of Christ "devoted themselves to the apostles' teaching.... Everyone was filled with awe, and many wonders and miraculous signs were done by the apostles. All the believers were together and had everything in common. Selling their possessions and goods, they gave to everyone as he had need."
- Acts 4:32-35 further emphasizes the radical economic practices of the early church: "All the believers were one in heart and mind. No claimed that any of his possessions was his own, but they shared everything they had. With great power the apostles continued to testify to the resurrection of the Lord Jesus, and much grace was upon them all. There were no needy persons among them. For from time to time those who owned lands or houses sold them, brought the money from the sales and put it at the apostles' feet, and it was distributed to anyone as he had need."

- In Galatians 3:26-28 Paul wrote: "You are all children of God through faith in Christ Jesus.... There is neither Jew nor Gentile, slave nor free, male nor female, for you are all one in Christ Jesus" – to which he could have added: "In Christ there is neither "black or brown or white," nor "rich or poor...." Christians should reject traditional classism, the mentality that honors the rich, the powerful and the socially-prominent at the expense of the poor, the common masses, and marginalized elements in society.
- Perhaps most notably, in II Corinthians 8:14 Paul exhorted the Christians in Corinth to share generously with the poor Christians in Macedonia: "Our desire is not that others might be relieved while you are hard pressed, but that there might be equality. At the present time your plenty will supply what they need, so that in turn their plenty will supply what you need. Then there will be equality, as it is written: 'He who gathered much did not have too much, and he who gathered little did not have too little'" [ref. Exodus 16:18]. Without turning this principle into some kind of legalistic mandate, it is nonetheless clear that Paul advocated a kind of Spirit-led social justice discipleship in which wealthier Christians shared their financial resources with less fortunate brothers and sisters in Christ based on sincere love and concern for their well-being. This is the essence of Christian charity and benevolence. But of course this has nothing to do with the kind of secular socialism in which the government confiscates wealth through forced taxation in order to redistribute it according to the preferences of the governing class or, as is often the case in democratic societies, to buy the votes of the underclass.

Beginning in the 1800s in Great Britain, America, and other predominantly Protestant nations, a wide range of social and humanitarian reforms, often initiated and promoted by Christians, resulted in new laws and regulations that provided some relief for

the struggling and often exploited working classes. These provisions, often advocated under the labels of Populism or Progressivism, initiated a mild form of democratic socialism. Some of the more notable reforms included:
- Humane prison reforms
- More humane treatment of the mentally retarded
- The abolition of slavery
- Women's rights
- More democratic, more efficient, and less corrupt government
- Governmental regulation of large corporations, monopolies and trusts
- Minimum wage laws
- A healthier, safer, and more humane work environment
- The rights of workers to unionize
- Limitations on the workday and workweek
- Decent working conditions for women and the abolition of child labor
- Pension plans for workers
- Old age and disability compensation

However, as Lewis notes, by the turn of the Twentieth Century the socialist ideal had been co-opted and corrupted. Beginning in Russia, militant Bolsheviks overthrew the tsarist regime and established a Communist dictatorship under the leadership of sadistic tyrants such as Vladimir Lenin and Leon Trotsky (and later, Josef Stalin). Meanwhile, rival left-wing factions wrestled for control in other countries, resulting in the triumph of Fascism in Italy under Benito Mussolini and the Nazi Party (National Socialist German Workers Party) under Adolf Hitler. All were militant atheists, all were morally bankrupt, all were ruthless totalitarians, and all were mass murderers.*

---

* One of the most pernicious deceptions of the Twentieth Century was the myth that Communism and Nazism (and its ally, Fascism) were polar opposite ideologies. In fact, despite being rival political movements, their similarities far exceeded their differences. To use conventional terminology, both were extreme "left-wing" totalitarian parties, the opposite of *[continued on the next page]*

Meanwhile, in democratic Britain, the left-wing Labour Party, operating under the benign guise of "democratic socialism," gained support especially among the lower classes by promoting an agenda based on "social equality" and the redistribution of wealth. Such a system, of course, requires a drastic increase in the size and the scope of government, which in turn leads to an increasingly intrusive and coercive government capable of effecting the mass redistribution of wealth via confiscatory taxation. Lewis understood that as such governments extend their power and control over more and more aspects of modern life, they inevitably over-regulate economic enterprises and social and cultural institutions along with the public and the private lives of their citizens. Eventually, they will also extend their authoritarian control over not only public institutions but churches and other private institutions.

Influenced as they are by classical Marxist ideology, democratic socialists have a simplistic understanding of social and economic history. In effect, their tendency is to put the economic "cart before the horse" by focusing more on the *redistribution* of wealth (goods and services) rather than incentivizing the *production* of wealth. But socialistic centralized planning simply does not work – economic systems and relationships are far too complex to be micro-managed by government bureaucrats. Furthermore, socialist policies are unjust and unfair: While promoting dependency and irresponsibility among the recipients of public assistance, socialism functions on the basis of the forced confiscation of a significant portion of the incomes of employers and employees.

* *[continued]* which would be the "right-wing" ideology of conservatism or far-right libertarianism that advocates for minimalist government.

As in *Dymer*, the aforementioned epic poem that he wrote early in his academic career, Lewis occasionally integrated social and political commentary into some of his fictional works. Most notably, Lewis' 1946 dystopian novel, *That Hideous Strength*, effectively dramatized the interaction of the two forces that he most feared: profit- and technology-driven corporate capitalism and authoritarian-style state socialism. In the preface Lewis notes that the story portrays in fictional terms a major concern that he earlier addressed in *The Abolition of Man*, namely: "[T]he power of Man to make himself what he pleases means... the power of some men to make other men what *they* please." As the novel unfolds, Lewis unveils his fear that Great Britain will become "developed" and ruined by a demonic alliance of greedy capitalists and soulless technocrats who care nothing for its natural beauty or historical heritage. In perhaps the book's defining paragraph, he lays out the ominous consequences of this axis of evil in terms that seem to presage not only contemporary postmodern relativism and the collapse of traditional Christian values but also the emerging new age of artificial intelligence, robotics and transhumanism.

> The physical sciences, good and innocent in themselves, had already, in Ransom's own time, begun to be warped, had been subtly manoeuvered in a certain direction. Despair of [i.e., skepticism of] objective truth had been increasingly insinuated into the scientists; indifference to it, and concentration upon mere power, had been the result.... Dreams of the far future destiny of man were dragging up from its shallow and unquiet grave the old dream of Man as God [ref. Genesis 3:1-5]. The very experiences of the dissecting room and the pathological laboratory were breeding a conviction that the stifling of all deep-set repugnancies [i.e., traditional values, Judeo-Christian morality, etc.] was the first essential for progress.... What should they find incredible, since they believed no longer in a rational universe? What should they regard as too obscene since they held that all morality

was a mere subjective by-product of the physical and economic situations of men? [The cumulative effects of Darwinism, Marxism and Freudianism.] The time was ripe. From the point of view which is accepted in Hell, the whole history of our Earth had led up to this moment. There was now at last a real chance for fallen Man to shake off that limitation of his powers which mercy had imposed upon him as a protection from the full results of the fall. If this succeeded, Hell would be at last incarnate. Bad men, while still in the body, still crawling on this little globe, would enter that state which, heretofore, they had entered only after death, would have the diuternity and power of evil spirits. Nature, all over the globe of Tellus, would become their slave; and of that dominion no end, before the end of time itself, could be certainly foreseen. [C. S. Lewis, *That Hideous Strength*, pp. 203-4.]

A dozen years later, in 1958, Lewis focused on the ominous nexus of state socialism and technocracy in an article entitled "Is Progress Possible? Willing Slaves of the Welfare State," the theme being "the changed relation between Government and its subjects [citizens]" in the post-Christian West, and the emergence of a "world Welfare State." In this global New World Order (as it has been labeled in more recent times), the masses willingly sacrifice personal freedom and autonomy in exchange for government-provided security (as in "Medicare for all" and defining healthcare insurance as a fundamental human "right"). According to Lewis, the future is unsettling as an ever-expanding Welfare State, working in conjunction with the "experts" of a "global technocracy," gradually expands its power over virtually every area of life. Lewis' dire warning is as succinct as it is emphatic: "I dread government in the name of science. That is how tyrannies come in."*

[Note: Consider the cumulative social, cultural, economic, political and spiritual effects of Karl Marx's "scientific socialism,"

---

* C. S. Lewis, "Is Progress Possible: Willing Slaves of the Welfare State," in Walter Hooper, ed., *God in the Dock,* p. 315.

Darwinian evolutionary theory, Nazi race theory, the modern eugenics movement, and the abortion industry. In more democratic nations, this is the *Brave New World* that Aldous Huxley envisioned. In more authoritarian states, it is George Orwell's *1984*. In *Brave New World*, citizens voluntarily surrender their civil liberties in exchange for personal hedonism and government-guaranteed security – what the Neo-Marxist social philosopher Herbert Marcuse labeled "libertarian socialism". In *1984* people are subjugated by a ruthless totalitarian state that controls every aspect of their lives. In either scenario, the technology/industrial complex – typified today by corporate behemoths such as Microsoft, Apple, Google, Facebook, Twitter, etc. – ultimately prevails.]

Although this government-regulated corporate and technology axis purports to be "progressive," in fact it threatens true progress. As Lewis explains in "Is Progress Possible: Willing Slaves of the Welfare State," true progress means "increasing goodness and happiness of individual lives," which requires freedom, virtue, and responsible citizenship. Furthermore, real progress in life implies that we proceed resolutely on a path that leads to that which is True, Good, and Beautiful. Ultimately, of course, that path culminates in God. Otherwise, as Lewis points out in this excerpt from *Mere Christianity*: we are merely deceiving ourselves,

> We all want progress. But progress means getting nearer to the place you want to be and if you have taken a wrong turning, then to go forward does not get you any nearer. If you are on the wrong road, progress means doing an about-turn and walking back to the right road; and in that case, the man who turns back soonest is the most progressive man....There is nothing progressive about being pigheaded and refusing to admit a mistake. And I think if you look at the present state of the world, it is pretty plain that humanity has been making some big mistakes. We are on the wrong road. And if that is so, we must go back. Going back is the quickest way on. [C. S. Lewis, *Mere Christianity*, pp. 28-29.]

With the realization that "Power corrupts, and absolute Power corrupts absolutely," Lewis asks rhetorically, "Have we discovered some new reason why, this time, power should not corrupt as it has done before?" But with the collapse of a consensus consciousness rooted in Natural Law, classical liberal ideology, and influenced by the Christian faith, modern man in the age of democratic socialism is forfeiting much of his independence. Like immature and dependent children, many in contemporary society are more than willing to forfeit personal privacy and freedom for government-guaranteed security in an increasingly technocratic and paternalistic "nanny" state.* This constitutes, according to Lewis, the "real dilemma" of our modern age:

> Two wars necessitated vast curtailments of liberty, and we have grown, though grumblingly, accustomed to our chains. The increasing complexity and precariousness of our economic life have forced Government to take over many spheres of activity once left to choice or chance....
>
> As a result, classical political theory [i.e., classical liberalism], with its Stoical, Christian, and juristic key conceptions (natural law, the value of the individual, the rights of man), has died. The modern State exists not to protect our rights but to do us good or make us good.... There is nothing left of which we can say to them, "Mind your own business." Our whole lives are their business....

---

* A major consequence of the modern welfare state, unforeseen by Lewis and other social observers in the 1940s and '50s, was the subsequent explosion in the illegitimate birth rate. Beginning in the late 1960s as a result of Lyndon John's Great Society that drastically increased the nation's welfare programs, millions of unwed mothers turned to the federal government (i.e., American taxpayers) for financial support for themselves and their children. Public charity soon came to be redefined as an "entitlement," and in many households welfare dependency became a lifestyle, in some cases subsequently perpetuated over the course of multiple generations, as Uncle Sam assumed the role of a surrogate (howbeit, an absentee and unfit) husband and father.

> As a result, classical political theory [i.e., classical liberalism], with its Stoical, Christian, and juristic key conceptions (natural law, the value of the individual, the rights of man), has died. The modern State exists not to protect our rights but to do us good or make us good.... There is nothing left of which we can say to them, "mind your own business." Our whole lives are their business....
>
> Here, I think, lies our real dilemma.... We are tamed animals (some with kind [democratic], some with cruel [totalitarian] masters and should probably starve if we got out of our cage.... [I]n an increasingly planned society, how much of what I value can survive? [C. S. Lewis,"Is Progress Possible?" pp. 313*ff.*]

Lewis continues with an impassioned plea for economic liberty, which is an integral component of classical liberal ideology and a necessary element of "the freeborn mind" in the same sense that intellectual, religious, political, social and vocational self-determination are essential to human flourishing.

> I believe a man is happier, and happy in a richer way, if he has "the freeborn mind." But I doubt whether he can have this without economic independence, which the new society is abolishing. For economic independence allows an education not controlled by the Government; and in adult life it is the [mature] man who needs, and asks, nothing of Government who can criticize its acts and [reject] its ideology.... Who will talk like that when the State is everyone's schoolmaster and employer? [Ibid.]

Lewis concludes this essay by asking rhetorically: "The question about progress has become the question whether we can discover any way of submitting to the worldwide paternalism of technocracy without losing all personal privacy and independence."

C. S. Lewis never claimed to have the gift of prophecy. Nonetheless, contemporary readers of his works on Natural Law, political philosophy and the Good Society can only marvel at his prescience. Undoubtedly, the United Kingdom, the United States and the rest of the world would be much healthier, happier, vibrant and wholesome societies had his warnings been heeded. But as Lewis would be the first to acknowledge, none of his insights were original or unique. He was merely a modern-day watchman reiterating the timeless principles of Truth, Goodness, and Beauty that he assimilated from a lifetime of immersion in the wisdom of the ages – and most prominently, the wisdom of Holy Scripture.

THE SUMMA

Lewisian Political Philosophy

In this study I have endeavored to set out as clearly and accurately as possible the observations, insights and recommended guidelines for responsible Christian citizenship as presented by C. S. Lewis in his writings. For Lewis, as for all thoughtful Christians who strive to integrate their faith and convictions into a comprehensive Christian worldview, politics matters because the laws, the policies and the programs of government significantly impact the quality-of-life for its citizens for better or for worse. Therefore, Lewis took the matter seriously and wrote substantially on various aspects of this vast and complex topic. The fact that it constitutes only a small fraction of his literary output does not minimize its importance.

For Lewis, a rational understanding of the proper role and scope of government and the social responsibility of Christians begins with traditional Natural Law – the moral foundation for social and political civility. As discussed in Part I, Natural Law functions as a baseline for morality and ethics, and as such it establishes reasonable standards of conduct for all citizens regardless of their religion, social class, sex or race. Without specifying how a just and prudent political system should be structured, the principles of Natural Law nonetheless express the fundamental rights and responsibilities of all citizens.

Traditional Christian moral teaching calls the followers of Jesus Christ to considerably higher standards of personal conduct than the tenets associated with Natural Law. These biblical principles, however, are for those who have voluntarily committed their lives to the Lordship of Christ, and as such they cannot and should not be forced on non-Christians. Any kind of theocratic and sacralistic imperialism violates the spirit of the Gospel – or as Lewis wrote: "Theocracy is the worst of all [possible] governments."

Part II: "The Political Philosophy of C. S. Lewis" began by clarifying the common misconception that Lewis had little or no interest in politics, and proceeded to highlight his most explicit writings on the subject. As a Christian moral philosopher, Lewis recognized the inherent evil in all totalitarian regimes, including both Soviet Bolshevism and German Nazism. He also opposed state socialism, whether it be classical Marxist Communism or Neo-Marxist "democratic socialism".

Lewis strove to set forth a vision for a rational, ethical and realistic political philosophy on the bases of Natural Law ethics and Classical Liberal theory as conceptualized primarily by the English political philosopher John Locke. This is the essence of republican-style government, which Lewis regarded as the best of all possible options. In that regard, Lewis was appropriately skeptical of the kind of democracy that had emerged in Great Britain, America, and other Western nations in the Nineteenth and Twentieth Centuries. For Lewis, democracy is a lowest-common-denominator form of government based on the modern sacrosanct myth of "equality" that rewards mediocrity and social conformity.

As Lewis envisioned, modern man in democratic societies is faced with two great challenges to true progress: (1) "Technocracy" – a scientific- and technology-industrial complex that threatens to dominate our lives; and (2) the emergence of a socialistic "World Welfare State" in which people's lives are increasingly controlled by government and dependent upon it for their basic needs and desires. As John West observes in his essay, "Finding the Permanent in the Political: C. S. Lewis as a Political Thinker," Lewis was most concerned about the tyranny that could result from the union of modern science and the modern state.

Part III: "Ruminations on the Good Society" focuses primarily on Book III, Chapter 3 of *Mere Christianity* in which Lewis set forth some ethical guidelines and policies for what he envisioned as a just society and government based on the principles of Natural Law, and how these concepts would influence and regulate the social and political systems in a relatively harmonious, well-functioning and healthy society. As emphasized in this section, Lewis' concept of a generically "good" society would not be a sacralistic Christian society in which the higher moral and ethical principles of the New Testament are coercively imposed on the general populace.

A Good Society would be in some respects "conservative" in terms of respecting and upholding certain traditional values and standards of decency (including traditional sexual mores). It would also promote the moral concept of "Good Work" and require individual responsibility while discouraging dependence on the government – or in Lewis' words, there would be "no passengers and no parasites." Conversely, the Good Society would also be in some respects "socialistic" in the idealistic sense of a society based on cooperation rather than radical individualism and ruthless competition. In that regard it would be a generous and charitable society that promotes the common good over purely individualistic rights. As noted, Lewis wrote in the epilogue of *The Screwtape Letters* that Nineteenth Century Christian socialism posed "the greatest threat to the kingdom of darkness in this world" before the socialist ideal was co-opted and corrupted by totalitarian-minded secularists such as Karl Marx and others.

Lewis, however, was certainly not naive regarding the inherent dangers of socialism as exemplified by those politicians and bureaucrats of the British Labour Party (and by extension, the modern Democratic Party in America) who strive to expand the power of government under labels such as "liberalism" and "progressivism" so as to increase their control over the lives of citizens. Exploiting class envy, group identify, racial tensions, and the inherent greed within individuals, these charlatans promote their agenda under the guise of "social justice" by expanding the welfare/entitlement state and promoting a radical redistribution of wealth. (*"Free healthcare, free housing, free college education, and a guaranteed annual income for all – including illegal immigrants!"*)

Regarding the alarming expansion of government and its control over the lives of its citizens since World War II, one of Lewis' most significant political writings was his 1958 article, "Is Progress Possible: Willing Slaves of the Welfare State," in which he asked rhetorically: "With the realization that 'Power corrupts, and absolute Power corrupts absolutely,' have we discovered some new reason why, this time, power should not corrupt as it has done before?" Clearly not. According to Lewis, this constitutes "the real dilemma" of our modern age – how to protect and preserve the individuality of citizens as free and autonomous beings while simultaneously imposing more government regulations and restrictions on their civil liberties. In an age such as ours in which the allied forces of fascistic Political Correctness are aggressively marginalizing, stifling and outright persecuting Christians, conservatives and even some liberals who resist their radical agenda, Lewis' hostility toward Big Brother government is even more relevant today than when he originally wrote it.

Onward: Our Calling as Christian Citizens

C. S. Lewis was one of the Twentieth Century's most perceptive moral thinkers, and it should not be surprising that he often turned his attention toward political philosophy and the proper role and scope of government. As with all his writings, contemporary Christians could learn much from his insights, admonitions and warnings. The issue remains, however, how we might faithfully apply this wisdom to our current political culture. In such a fallen and dysfunctional world, the parameters of our citizenship responsibilities as conscientious Christians and the extent of our political engagement can be complicated and perplexing.

In essence, Christianity is a spiritual relationship with God through faith in Jesus Christ and the indwelling presence of the Holy Spirit. Christianity is also a religion, but it is more than affirming certain doctrines and practices and observing traditional rites and rituals. Christianity is also more than personal piety. In its fullest dimension, Christianity is a comprehensive worldview that should condition and regulate not only our theological beliefs and moral sensibilities but how we think and respond to the full range of life issues – or what Francis Schaeffer referred to as "the lordship of Christ over the whole of life." As citizens of a free country and a social community built on democratic principles of participatory government, we have responsibilities that far exceed those of the early Christians to whom the apostolic writings of the New Testament were addressed.

Whether we prefer to acknowledge it or not, politics and government matter. Regrettably, many Christians have been led to believe that we should be as apolitical as possible so as to eliminate any unnecessary distractions or impediments in our witness to others. After all, they say, what really matters is the Gospel. The implication of the argument is that politics is messy, unspiritual and divisive, so for the sake of our Christian testimony we should stay focused on "things above" rather than worldly concerns. They argue that politics is mostly about the acquisition (and often the abuse) of earthly power, and most politicians are little more than proverbial "pigs at the trough."

But this is actually quite naive. Although it may not be true that "everything is political," much in life certainly is. For example, both the early Christians and their state-approved persecutors were quick to realize that there is no more "political" statement than the declaration, "Jesus is Lord!"

America's Founding Fathers recognized that politics is a necessary component of life and that laws and public policies are based either on the universal moral and ethical principles of justice derived from Natural Law or else the arbitrary and tyrannical applications of coercion by the power elite over everyone else. They understood that laws and public policies can either enhance or detract from the quality of one's life, liberty, and pursuit of happiness. Furthermore, they were mindful that political ignorance, apathy and non-involvement only empowers the most ambitious and ruthless elements in society. In other words, they understood that politics matters.

When asked, "Rabbi, which is the greatest commandment in the Law?" Jesus replied: "'Love the Lord your God with all your heart, soul, mind, and passion. This is the greatest commandment. And the second is like it: 'Love your neighbor as yourself'" – i.e., "Treat others in the same way that you would want them to treat you" (Matt. 22:36-39). Now the question is simply this: How can we possibly love others if we are indifferent regarding the kinds of laws and public policies that regulate (and often control) their lives? How can we truly love others unless we are sensitive and attentive not only to their religious and spiritual lives but their physical, material, emotional, social, intellectual and creative needs as well?

Realistically, we know that everything fallible human beings do is imperfect. Everything manmade, including all our social, economic, political, educational and religious systems and institutions, are shades of grey. Therefore, the first guiding principle of responsible citizenship should be: It is mostly about damage-control, and it often comes down to keeping the very *worst* people with the *worst* intentions out of positions of power and influence. No manmade political party or ideology has a monopoly on truth, reason and wisdom, and it is rare that citizens ever have an opportunity to vote for an ideal candidate. But it is simplistic, foolish and dangerous to assume that because all candidates, parties and ideologies are flawed, therefore they are all morally equivalent. In reality, some are far more rational, ethical and wise than others. To ignore the differences and pretend otherwise is irresponsible and tantamount to willful ignorance.

Politics is not ultimately what matters most in this life, nor is it the answer to mankind's deepest needs. The Gospel is. But as Jesus clearly taught, the Main Thing is not the Only Thing. (To paraphrase Matthew 22:15-21 – "Give to the government what rightfully belongs to the government, and unto God the things that are God's.") To truly love others as we love ourselves, there is a political component that cannot be denied. We must care deeply about the kind of society and culture in which we and others live, and to ignore the political implications of wholistic Christian discipleship is not only irresponsible but immoral. Because politics is an integral part of life, we have a moral responsibility to be well-informed and actively-engaged in the great issues of our time. Otherwise, as the British statesman Edmund Burke famously put it: "All that is necessary for the triumph of evil is that good men [and women] do nothing."

The common "secular v. sacred" dichotomy is an artificial contrivance. A truly Christian worldview is comprehensive, incorporating every area of life. For devout followers of Jesus Christ, their faith should inform and regulate all their priorities, obligations and involvements. In an essay Lewis wrote at the outset of World War II, "Learning in Wartime" (1939), he was careful to distinguish between the allegiance one owes to one's nation and that which one owes to God. "A man may have to die for [his] country," he explains, "but no man must, in any exclusive sense, live for his country." That being the case, "He who surrenders himself without reservation to the temporal claims of a nation, or a [political] party, or a [social] class is rendering to Caesar that which, of all things, most emphatically belongs to God: himself."*

Six years later as the war drew to a close, Lewis wrote another essay entitled "Membership" in which he reminded his readers that what matters most is not the nation-state but the spiritual state of the individual. As he noted, "It was not for societies or states that Christ

---

* C. S. Lewis, "Learning in Wartime," in Walter Hooper, ed., *The Weight of Glory and Other Addresses*, p. 53.

died, but for man[kind]."* There will come a time when every civilization, every nation, every culture, and every institution will become extinct, yet each individual will still exist as a living soul. Therefore, as Lewis had emphasized in his wartime radio broadcasts (and later incorporated into *Mere Christianity*), we must reject the secular tendency to value society or the state over individuals:

> If individuals live only 70 years or so, then a nation or a civilization is more important than the individual, for it could last a thousand years.... But if Christianity is true, then the individual is not only more important but incomparably more important, for he is everlasting.
> [C. S. Lewis, *Mere Christianity*, pp. 74-75]

This is a theme that Lewis returned to in one of his last works, "Screwtape Proposes a Toast" (1961). Assuming the role of a senior demon instructing his subordinates on the proper means by which they might most effectively confuse and defeat the humans to whom they have been assigned, he imparts sage (if Satanic) advice:

> You must convince your "human victims" of the delusion "that the fate of nations is in itself more important than that of individual souls. The overthrow of free peoples and multiplication of [totalitarian] slave-states are for us a means [to an end] – besides, of course being fun; but the real end is the destruction of individuals. For only individuals can be saved or damned, can become sons of the Enemy [God] or food for us. The ultimate value, for us, of any revolution, war, or famine lies in the individual anguish, treachery, hatred, rage, and despair which it may produce. [The democratic mantra of "equality"] is a useful means for the destruction of democratic societies. But it has far deeper value as an end in itself, as a state of mind, which... turns a human being away from almost every road which might finally lead him to Heaven.
> [C. S. Lewis, *The Screwtape Letters*, 207-8.]

---

* C. S. Lewis, "Membership," in Walter Hooper, ed., *The Weight of Glory and Other Addresses*, p. 172.

In summation, Lewis' essentially would have agreed with the French Christian philosopher Jacques Maritain (1882-1973) that the calling of the Christian in society is not primarily that of a partisan but a social prophet and a watchman on the wall. This was also the conclusion of Jacques Ellul, who argued in *The Subversion of Christianity* (published posthumously in 1987) that the role of the Christian in society is to question – and when appropriate, challenge – the political powers that be. But we must also understand that the Christian's role as a countercultural watchman entails far more than being merely a critical observer. In no way does it excuse us from active involvement in the great moral and ethical battles that are currently raging in our contemporary culture war.

Ultimately, C. S. Lewis cared about the relationship between government and its citizens because political systems, laws and policies can either help or hinder individuals in realizing their *telos* – their God-given purpose, potential and goal in life. In that regard, we must strive to be informed, vigilant and active when it comes to exposing and defeating those most pernicious lies – and the political advocates of such lies – that pose the greatest threats to what is...

True
Factual and rational

Good
Moral and ethical

and

Beautiful
Inspiring and edifying

Lewis understood that as faithful followers of Jesus Christ, every Christian is called to be a source of Light, Love and Truth. If we truly love God with all our heart, soul, mind and strength – and if we endeavor to love others as we love ourselves – surely we will prioritize our time, our energy and our resources so as to fulfill our calling in this life for the ultimate glory of God.

APPENDIX

Sources Cited

Jefrey D. Breshears, *Natural Law: The Moral Foundation for Social and Political Civility* (CentrePointe Publishing, 2016).

_____ "What's Wrong With Socialism" (www.TheAreopagus.org).

Justin Buckley Dyer and Micah J. Watson, *C. S. Lewis on Politics and the Natural Law* (Cambridge University Press, 2016).

J. Budziszewski, *What We Can't Not Know* (Spence Publishing Company, 2003).

Aldous Huxley, *Brave New World* (Chatto & Windless, 1932).

Martin Luther King, Jr. "Letter from a Birmingham Jail" (https://web.cn.edu/kwheeler/documents/Letter_Birmingham_Jail.pdf)

C. S. Lewis, "Dymer" (1926), published in *C. S. Lewis, Narrative Poems* (HarperOne – Reprint Edition, 2017).

_____ "Why I Am Not a Pacifist" (1939), published in Walter Hooper, ed., *The Weight of Glory and Other Addresses* (William Collins, 2013).

_____ "Learning in Wartime (1939), published in *The Weight of Glory and Other Addresses* (William Collins, 2013).

_____ *Mere Christianity* – Book III, Chapter 3 on "Social Morality" (HarperSanFrancisco, 1952, 1980).

_____ *The Abolition of Man* (HarperSanFrancisco, 1944).

_____ "Bulverism: The Foundation of 20th Century Thought" (1944), published in *God in the Dock: Essays on Theology and Ethics* (William B. Eerdmans Publishing Co., 1970).

_____ *That Hideous Strength* (1945) – Book III in the Space Trilogy (Macmillan Publishing Company, 1965).

_____ "Membership" (1945), published in Walter Hooper, ed., *The Weight of Glory and Other Addresses* (William Collins, 2013).

_____ "Christian Apologetics" (1945), published in Walter Hooper, ed., *God in the Dock: Essays on Theology and Ethics* (William B. Eerdmans Publishing, 1970).

———— "God in the Dock" (1948), published in Walter Hooper, ed., *God in the Dock: Essays on Theology and Ethics* (William B. Eerdmans Publishing Company, 1970).

———— "A Reply to Professor Haldane" (1956), published in Walter Hooper, ed., *Of Other Worlds: Essays and Stories* (Harcourt Brace Jovanovich, 1966).

———— "Is Progress Possible? Willing Slaves of the Welfare State" (1958), published in *God in the Dock: Essays on Theology and Ethics* (William B. Eerdmans Publishing Company, 1970).

———— "Screwtape Proposes a Toast" (1959), an epilogue to *The Screwtape Letters* (HarperSanFrancisco, 1942, 1996).

Warren Lewis, ed., *Letters of C. S. Lewis* (Harcourt, 1966).

Herbert Marcuse, *Eros and Civilization* (Beacon Press, 1955).

Gilbert Meilander, *The Taste for the Other: The Social and Ethical Thought of C. S. Lewis* (William B. Eerdmans Publishing Company, 1978).

George Orwell, *1984* (Secker & Warburg, 1949).

George Sayer, *Jack: A Life of C. S. Lewis* (Crossway Books, 1988, 1994).

E. F. Schumacher, *Good Work* (Harper & Row Publishers, 1979)

John G. West, "Finding the Permanent in the Political: C. S. Lewis as a Political Thinker" (https://www.discovery.org/a/457/#).

C. S. Lewis
A Selected Bibliography

David Baggett, Gary R. Habermas, and Jerry L. Walls, eds., *C. S. Lewis as Philosopher: Truth, Goodness and Beauty* (IVP Academic, 2008).

John Beversluis, *C. S. Lewis and the Search for Rational Religion* (Eerdmans, 1985).

John Beversluis, "Beyond the Double-Bolted Door." *Christian History* (Vol. 4, No. 3, 1985), pp. 28-31.

John Beversluis, "Surprised by Freud: A Critical Appraisal of A. N. Wilson's Biography of C. S. Lewis." *Christianity and Literature* (Vol. 41, No. 2, 1992), pp. 179-95.

Humphrey Carpenter, *The Inklings* (Allen & Unwin, 1978).

Christopher Derrick, *C. S. Lewis and the Church of Rome* (Ignatius Press, 1981).

Christopher Derrick, "Putting C. S. Lewis On the Couch." *New Oxford Review* (May, 1990).

David C. Downing, *Into the Region of Awe: Mysticism in C. S. Lewis* (IVP, 2005).

Justin Buckley Dyer and Micah J. Watson, *C. S. Lewis on Politics and the Natural Law* (Cambridge University Press, 2016).

Paul Holmer, *C. S. Lewis: The Shape of His Faith and Thought* (Harper & Row, 1976).

Walter Hooper, ed., *God in the Dock: Essays on Theology and Ethics* (William B. Eerdmans Publishing Co., 1970).

Walter Hooper, ed., *The Weight of Glory and Other Addresses* (William Collins, 2013)

Walter Hooper, *C. S. Lewis: A Complete Guide to His Life and Works* (HarperOne, 1998).

Thomas Howard and Peter Kreeft, *Narnia and Beyond: A Guide to the Fiction of C. S. Lewis* (Ignatius Press, 2006).

Clyde Kilby, *The Christian World of C. S. Lewis* (Eerdmans, 1995).

Peter Kreeft, *C. S. Lewis For the Third Millennium* (Ignatius Press, 1994).

Peter Kreeft, "Lewis's Philosophy of Truth, Goodness and Beauty." Published in David Baggett, Gary R. Habermas, and Jerry L. Walls, eds., *C. S. Lewis as Philosopher: Truth, Goodness, and Beauty* (IVP Academic, 2008).

C. S. Lewis, "Dymer." Published in *C. S. Lewis, Narrative Poems* (HarperOne – Reprint Edition, 2017).

C. S. Lewis, "Why I Am Not a Pacifist." Published in Walter Hooper, ed., *The Weight of Glory and Other Addresses* (William Collins, 2013).

C. S. Lewis, "Learning in Wartime." Published in Walter Hooper, ed., *The Weight of Glory and Other Addresses* (William Collins, 2013).

C. S. Lewis, *The Problem of Pain* (HarperSanFrancisco, 1940).

C. S. Lewis, *The Abolition of Man* (HarperSanFrancisco, 1944).

C. S. Lewis, *The Great Divorce* (HarperSanFranciso, 1946).

C. S. Lewis, *Miracles* (HarperSanFrancisco, 1947).

C. S. Lewis, "Bulverism: The Foundation of 20th Century Thought." Published in Walter Hooper, ed., *God in the Dock: Essays on Theology and Ethics* (William B. Eerdmans Publishing Co., 1970).

C. S. Lewis, *That Hideous Strength* (Macmillan Publishing Company, 1965).

C. S. Lewis, *Mere Christianity* (HarperSanFrancisco, 1952).

C. S. Lewis, "Membership." Published in Walter Hooper, ed., *The Weight of Glory and Other Addresses* (William Collins, 2013).

C. S. Lewis, "Christian Apologetics." Published in Walter Hooper, ed., *God in the Dock: Essays on Theology and Ethics* (William B. Eerdmans Publishing, 1970).

C. S. Lewis, "God in the Dock." Published in Walter Hooper, ed., *God in the Dock: Essays on Theology and Ethics* (William B. Eerdmans Publishing Company, 1970).

C. S.Lewis, *Surprised by Joy: The Shape of My Early Life* (Harcourt, Inc., 1955).

C. S. Lewis, "Is Progress Possible? Willing Slaves of the Welfare State." Published in *God in the Dock: Essays on Theology and Ethics* (William B. Eerdmans Publishing Company, 1970).

C. S. Lewis, "A Reply to Professor Haldane." Published in *Of Other Worlds: Essays and Stories* (Harcourt Brace Jovanovich, 1975).

C. S. Lewis, "Screwtape Proposes a Toast." An epilogue to C. S. Lewis, *The Screwtape Letters* (HarperSanFrancisco, 1942, 1996).

Warren Lewis, ed., *Letters of C. S. Lewis* (Harcourt, 1966).

Art Lindsley, *C. S. Lewis's Case For Christ: Insights from Reason, Imagination and Faith* (IVP, 2005).

Louis A. Markos, "Myth Matters." *Christianity Today* (April 23, 2001).

Gilbert Meilander, *The Taste for the Other: The Social and Ethical Thought of C. S. Lewis* (William B. Eerdmans Publishing Company, 1978).

Victor Reppert, "Taking C. S. Lewis Seriously." *Books & Culture* (Sep/Oct 2003), pp. 12-15.

Victor Reppert, *C. S. Lewis's Dangerous Idea* (Inter-Varsity Press, 2003).

George Sayer, *Jack: C. S. Lewis and His Times* (Harper & Row, 1988).

Brian Sibley, *C. S. Lewis Through the Shadowlands* (Baker/Revell, 1999).

Sheldon Vanauken, "The Best Book Written About C. S. Lewis." *New Oxford Review* (Dec. 1988).

Chad Walsh, *Literary Legacy of C. S. Lewis* (Wipf & Stock, 2008).

A.N. Wilson, *C. S. Lewis: A Biography* (W. W. Norton, 1990).